A MIDSUMMER NIGHT'S DREAM

Shakespeare: The Animated Tales is a multinational venture conceived by S4C, Channel 4 Wales. Produced in Russia, Wales, and England, the series has been financed by S4C, the BBC, and HIT Communications (UK), Christmas Films and Soyuzmultfilm (Russia), Home Box Office (USA), and Fujisankei (Japan).

Academic Panel
Professor Stanley Wells
Dr. Rex Gibson

Academic Co-ordinator
Roy Kendall

Educational Adviser
Michael Marland

Publishing Editor and Co-ordinator
Jane Fior

Book Design
Fiona Macmillan

Animation Director for *A Midsummer Night's Dream*
Robert Saakianz of Christmas Joint Venture, Moscow

Series Producer and Director
Dave Edwards of The Dave Edwards Studio Ltd, Cardiff, Wales

Executive Producers
Christopher Grace
Elizabeth Babakhina

Library of Congress Cataloging-in-Publication Data
Garfield, Leon.
    A midsummer night's dream / abridged by Leon Garfield ; illustrated by Elena Prorokova.
        p.   cm. — (Shakespeare, the animated tales)
    Summary: An illustrated, abridged version of the Shakespeare comedy with background information and explanatory stage directions.
        ISBN 0–679–83870–8 (pbk.) — ISBN 0–679–93870–2 (lib. bdg.)
    1. Children's plays, English. [1. Plays.] I. Prorokova, Elena, ill.
II. Shakespeare, William, 1564–1616. Midsummer night's dream.
III. Title. IV. Series: Garfield, Leon. Shakespeare, the animated tales.
PR2827.A25   1993
822.3'3—dc20   92–14522

Shakespeare

A MIDSUMMER NIGHT'S DREAM

ABRIDGED BY LEON GARFIELD

ILLUSTRATED BY ELENA PROROKOVA

ALFRED A. KNOPF · NEW YORK

THE THEATRE IN SHAKESPEARE'S DAY

IN 1989 AN ARCHAEOLOGICAL discovery was made on the south bank of the Thames that sent shivers of delight through the theatre world. A fragment of Shakespeare's own theatre, the Globe, where many of his plays were first performed, had been found.

This discovery has fuelled further interest in how Shakespeare himself conceived and staged his plays. We know a good deal already, and archaeology as well as documentary research will no doubt reveal more, but although we can only speculate on some of the details, we have a good idea of what the Elizabethan theatre-goer saw, heard and smelt when he went to see a play by William Shakespeare at the Globe.

It was an entirely different experience from anything we know today. Modern theatres have roofs to keep out the weather. If it rained on the Globe, forty per cent of the play-goers got wet. Audiences today sit on cushioned seats, and usually (especially if the play is by Shakespeare) watch and listen in respectful silence. In the Globe, the floor of the theatre was packed with a riotous crowd of garlic-reeking apprentices, house servants and artisans, who had each paid a penny to stand for the entire duration of the play, to buy nuts and apples from the food-sellers, to refresh themselves with bottled ale, relieve themselves, perhaps, into buckets by the back wall, to talk, cheer, catcall, clap and hiss if the play did not please them.

In the galleries, that rose in curved tiers around the inside of the building, sat those who could afford to pay two pennies for a seat, and the benefits of a roof over their heads. Here, the middle ranking citizens, the merchants, the sea captains, the clerks from the Inns of Court, would sit crammed into their small eighteen inch space and look down upon the 'groundlings' below. In the 'Lords room', the rich and the great, noblemen and women, courtiers and foreign ambassadors had to pay sixpence each for the relative comfort and luxury of their exclusive position directly above the stage, where they smoked tobacco, and overlooked the rest.

We are used to a stage behind an arch, with wings on either side, from which the actors come on and into which they disappear. In the Globe, the stage was a platform thrusting out into the middle of the floor, and the audience, standing in the central yard, surrounded it on three sides. There were no wings. Three doors at the back of the stage were used for all exits and entrances. These were sometimes covered by a curtain, which could be used as a prop.

Today we sit in a darkened theatre or cinema, and look at a brilliantly lit stage or screen, or we sit at home in a small, private world of our own, watching a luminous television screen. The close-packed, rowdy crowd at the Globe, where the play started at two o'clock in the afternoon, had no artificial light to enhance their illusion. It was the words that moved them. They came to listen, rather than to see.

No dimming lights announced the start of the play. A blast from a trumpet and three sharp knocks warned the audience that the action was about to begin. In the broad daylight, the actor could see the audience as clearly as the audience could see him. He spoke directly to the crowd, and held them with his eyes, following their reactions. He could play up to the raucous laughter that greeted the comical, bawdy scenes, and gauge the emotional response to the higher flights of poetry. Sometimes he even improvised speeches of his own. He was surrounded by, enfolded by his audience.

The stage itself would seem uncompromisingly bare to our eyes. There was no scenery. No painted backdrops suggested a forest, or a castle, or the sumptuous interior of a palace. Shakespeare painted the scenery with his words, and the imagination of the audience did the rest.

Props were brought onto the stage only when they were essential for the action. A bed would be carried on when a character needed to lie on it. A throne would be let down from above when a king needed to sit on it. Torches and lanterns would suggest that it was dark, but the main burden of persuading an audience, at three o'clock in the afternoon, that it was in fact the middle of the night, fell upon the language. In *A Midsummer Night's Dream*, Shakespeare evokes the night with one line of verse, as Oberon addresses Titania: 'I'll met by moonlight, proud Titania!'

In our day, costume designers create a concept as part of the production of a play into which each costume fits. Shakespeare's actors were responsible for their own costumes. They would use what was to hand in the 'tiring house' (dressing room), or supplement it out of their own pockets. Classical, medieval and Tudor clothes could easily appear side by side in the same play.

No women actors appeared on a public stage until many years after Shakespeare's death, for at that time it would have been considered shameless. The parts of young girls were played by boys. The parts of older women were played by older men.

In 1613 the Globe theatre was set on fire by a spark from a cannon during a performance of Henry VIII, and it burnt to the ground. The actors, including Shakespeare himself, dug into their own pockets and paid for it to be rebuilt. The new theatre lasted until 1642, when it closed again. Now, in the 1990s, the Globe is set to rise again as a committed band of actors, scholars and enthusiasts are raising the money to rebuild Shakespeare's theatre in its original form a few yards from its previous site.

From the time when the first Globe theatre was built until today, Shakespeare's plays have been performed in a vast variety of languages, styles, costumes and techniques, on stage, on film, on television and in animated film. Shakespeare himself, working within the round wooden walls of his theatre, would have been astonished by it all.

Patrick Spottiswoode
Director Globe Education,
Shakespeare Globe Trust

WILLIAM SHAKESPEARE

NEXT TO GOD, A wise man once said, Shakespeare created most. In the thirty-seven plays that are his chief legacy to the world—and surely no-one ever left a richer!—human nature is displayed in all its astonishing variety.

He has enriched the stage with matchless comedies, tragedies, histories, and, towards the end of his life, with plays that defy all description, strange plays that haunt the imagination like visions.

His range is enormous: kings and queens, priests, princes and merchants, soldiers, clowns and drunkards, murderers, pimps, whores, fairies, monsters and pale, avenging ghosts 'strut and fret their hour upon the stage'. Murders and suicides abound; swords flash, blood flows, poison drips, and lovers sigh; yet there is always time for old men to talk of growing apples and for gardeners to discuss the weather.

In the four hundred years since they were written, they have become known and loved in every land; they are no longer the property of one country and one people, they are the priceless possession of the world.

His life, from what we know of it, was not astonishing. The stories that have attached themselves to him are remarkable only for their ordinariness: poaching deer, sleeping off a drinking bout under a wayside tree. There are no duels, no loud, passionate loves, no excesses of any kind. He was not one of your unruly geniuses whose habits are more interesting than their works. From all accounts, he was of a gentle, honourable disposition, a good businessman, and a careful father.

He was born on April 23rd 1564, to John and Mary Shakespeare of Henley Street, Stratford-upon-Avon. He was their third child and first son. When he was four or five he began his education at the local petty school. He left the local grammar school when he was about fourteen, in all probability to help in his father's glove-making shop. When he was eighteen, he married Anne Hathaway, who lived in a nearby village. By the time he was twenty-one, he was the father of three children, two daughters and a son.

Then, it seems, a restless mood came upon him. Maybe he travelled, maybe he was, as some say, a schoolmaster in the country; but at some time during the next seven years, he went to London and found employment in the theatre. When he was twenty-eight, he was already well enough known as an actor and playwright to excite the spiteful envy of a rival, who referred to him as 'an upstart crow'.

He mostly lived and worked in London until his mid-forties, when he returned to his family and home in Stratford, where he remained in prosperous circumstances until his death on April 23rd 1616, his fifty-second birthday.

He left behind him a widow, two daughters (his son died in childhood), and the richest imaginary world ever created by the human mind.

A Midsummer Night's Dream

Of all Shakespeare's plays, this must be the best-loved. It is the story of a night of confusions in a haunted wood. Four young lovers, trying to resolve their passions, and six worthy workmen, trying to rehearse a play, stumble about in its magical moonlight, while the powerful spirits of the wood, who have mysterious affairs of their own, play havoc with their hearts and minds.

It is the story of a magical flower whose juice plays strange tricks on the eyes, turning love to hate, and hate to love. It is the story of fools and fairies, and, above all, of Bottom, the weaver, whose head has been magically transformed into the head of an ass, and who, for the space of a glorious hour, finds himself in the arms of Titania, Queen of the Fairies, while Oberon, her dread lord, steals away her beloved Indian page.

Shakespeare wrote it at about the same time as *Romeo and Juliet,* when he was thirty-one or two; and indeed the two plays have much in common, one, at times, seeming almost the comic counterpart of the other.

It is a play about illusion and the transfiguring power of imagination. At the very beginning we are told that there is nothing to choose between two young men. 'I am, my lord, as well derived as he, as well possessed,' says one to the duke who is judging the case, 'my fortunes every way as fairly ranked.' But nonetheless, Hermia's father has chosen one, and Hermia herself has chosen the other. 'I would my father looked but with my eyes,' says Hermia;

while the duke advises, 'Rather your eyes must with his judgement look', leaving poor Hermia to wail hopelessly, 'O hell, to choose love by another's eyes!'

And then, in the midnight wood, eyes are bewitched; love turns to hatred, and scorn to breathless, panting love. Illusion reigns supreme; not even the Fairy Queen is spared, for she, her sight enchanted, sees in donkey-headed Bottom a being of matchless beauty.

And Bottom, who cannot see that he has an ass's head, suffers from the illusion—as do we all—that others see him as he supposes himself. Yet to Bottom, Bully Bottom, the best man in all Athens, must go the last word in summing up our feelings about this play. 'I have had a most rare vision,' he says; and so indeed have we.

LEON GARFIELD

The Characters in the Play
in order of appearance

Egeus	*Hermia's father*
Theseus	*Duke of Athens*
Hermia	*in love with Lysander*
Demetrius Lysander	*young courtiers, in love with Hermia*
Helena	*in love with Demetrius*
Peter Quince	*a carpenter, Prologue in the Interlude*
Nick Bottom	*a weaver, Pyramus in the Interlude*
Francis Flute	*a bellows-mender, Thisbe in the Interlude*
Snug	*a joiner, Lion in the Interlude*
Oberon	*King of the Fairies*
Titania	*Queen of the Fairies*
Puck	*Oberon's jester and lieutenant*
Attendants	*to Titania*
Tom Snout	*a tinker, Wall in the Interlude*
Hippolyta	*Queen of the Amazons, betrothed to Theseus*
Robin Starveling	*a tailor, Moonshine in the Interlude*
Philostrate	*Theseus' Master of the Revels*

The curtain rises on Athens, a white and golden city, bright and joyous as a wedding cake. Everywhere there is preparation for the marriage of Duke Theseus to Hippolyta, the queen he has won in battle. But in the midst of all this happiness, there is a speck of misery, like a sour plum . . .

Into the council chamber of the palace, an angry father, Egeus, drags his disobedient daughter, Hermia, to seek justice before the duke and his royal bride.

She will not marry the man of his choice but obstinately prefers another.

After them come the two young men in question: Lysander, the daughter's desire and Demetrius, her father's. Wilfully, she breaks free of Egeus's grasp.

EGEUS Happy be Theseus, our renowned Duke! Full of vexation come I, with complaint against my child, my daughter Hermia. Stand forth, Demetrius! (*Demetrius, full of virtue, stands forth.*) My noble lord, this man hath my consent to marry her. Stand forth, Lysander! (*Lysander, full of defiance, stands forth.*) And, my gracious Duke, this man hath bewitched the bosom of my child. (*Lysander and Hermia exchange ardent looks.*) Be it so she will not here, before your grace, consent to marry with Demetrius, I beg the ancient privilege of Athens; as she is mine, I may dispose of her, either to this gentleman or to her death.

THESEUS Be advised, fair maid. Demetrius is a worthy gentleman.

HERMIA So is Lysander. I do entreat your grace to pardon me. But I beseech your grace that I may know the worst that may befall me in this case, if I refuse to wed Demetrius.

THESEUS Either to die the death, or to abjure for ever the society of men. Take time to pause—

Hermia and Lysander gaze at each other.

DEMETRIUS Relent, sweet Hermia; and Lysander, yield—

LYSANDER

You have her father's love, Demetrius, let me have Hermia's —do you marry him. (*To the duke*) I am, my lord, as well-derived as he, and, which is more, I am beloved of beauteous Hermia. Demetrius, I'll avouch it to his head, made love to Nedar's daughter, Helena, and won her soul.

THESEUS

I must confess that I have heard so much. But Demetrius, come, and come, Egeus. You shall go with me. For you, fair Hermia, look you arm yourself to fit your fancies to your father's will.

They all depart, leaving Hermia and Lysander alone.

LYSANDER

Ay me! The course of true love never did run smooth.

HERMIA

If then true lovers have been ever crossed, it stands as an edict in destiny.

LYSANDER

So quick bright things come to confusion. If thou lov'st me, then steal forth thy father's house tomorrow night, and in the wood, a league without the town, there will I stay for thee.

HERMIA

I swear to thee by Cupid's strongest bow, tomorrow truly will I meet with thee.

LYSANDER

Keep promise, love. Look, here comes Helena!

Helena enters, much distracted, for she loves Demetrius even as Hermia loves Lysander but alas with no return.

HERMIA   God speed, fair Helena! Whither away?

HELENA   Call you me fair? That 'fair' again unsay. O teach me how you look, and with what art you sway the motion of Demetrius' heart.

HERMIA   Take comfort: he no more shall see my face.

LYSANDER   Tomorrow night through Athens' gates have we devised to steal.

HERMIA   And in the wood where often you and I were wont to lie, there my Lysander and myself shall meet. Farewell, sweet playfellow; pray thou for us!

They all part. Helena lingers and gazes bitterly after Hermia.

HELENA   Ere Demetrius looked on Hermia's eyne, he hailed down oaths that he was only mine. I will go tell him of fair Hermia's flight! (*Vindictively*) Then to the wood . . .

So while the preparations for the wedding of Duke Theseus occupy his subjects, the four lovers flee the city. Meanwhile, in a humble, smoky, candlelit room, six worthy workmen of Athens are gathered together. They are to prepare a play for the festivities of the wedding. If they succeed, they will all be given pensions for life; so it is a serious business. The play has been chosen: it is Pyramus and Thisbe, a tale of tragic lovers.

The company is to be directed by Peter Quince, the carpenter. Foremost among his actors is Nick Bottom, the weaver. The lesser lights are Flute, the bellows-mender, Snout, the tinker, Snug, the joiner, and Starveling, the tailor.

QUINCE   Is all our company here? (*They nod.*) Here is the scroll of every man's name which is thought fit through all Athens to play in our interlude before the Duke and Duchess on his wedding day at night. Answer me as I call you. Nick Bottom, the weaver?

BOTTOM   Ready. Name what part I am for, and proceed.

QUINCE   You, Nick Bottom, are set down for Pyramus.

BOTTOM   What is Pyramus? A lover or a tyrant?

QUINCE   A lover that kills himself, most gallant, for love. Francis Flute, the bellows-mender?

FLUTE   Here, Peter Quince.

QUINCE   Flute, you must take Thisbe on you.

FLUTE   Nay, faith, let me not play a woman: I have a beard coming.

QUINCE   That's all one: you shall play it in a mask—

BOTTOM   Let me play Thisbe too—

QUINCE   No, no; you must play Pyramus; and Flute, you Thisbe. Robin Starveling, the tailor? You must play Thisbe's mother. Tom Snout, the tinker? You, Pyramus' father; myself, Thisbe's father; Snug, the joiner, you the lion's part.

SNUG   Have you the lion's part written? Pray you, if it be, give it to me, for I am slow of study.

QUINCE   You may do it extempore; for it is nothing but roaring.

BOTTOM   Let me play the lion too. I will roar that I will make the Duke say, 'Let him roar again!'

QUINCE   You can play no part but Pyramus; for Pyramus is a sweet-faced man.

BOTTOM   Well, I will undertake it.

QUINCE   Here are your parts, (*he distributes scrolls*) and I am to entreat you to con them by tomorrow night, and meet me in the palace wood by moonlight; there will we rehearse . . .

The wood. The moon shines down and tips all the leaves with silver. It is a place of mystery. Unseen creatures rustle among the bushes, like disturbed dreams. Suddenly, in a clearing, a weird configuration of tree and leaf becomes a strange, threatening figure in a dark cloak. It is Oberon, king of the night-time world. At his feet crouches Puck, his wicked, grinning henchman, and all about are his sharp-eyed goblin servants.

OBERON   Ill met by moonlight, proud Titania.

Across the glade appears the delicate, glittering fairy queen, accompanied by her glimmering train of sprites. Among them is a pretty little Indian boy, guarded like a jewel. The fairy king and queen stare at one another with hostility.

TITANIA   What, jealous Oberon? Fairies, skip hence! I have forsworn his bed and company. (*She raises her hand. Her followers quiver and tremble to depart.*)

OBERON   Tarry, rash wanton! Why should Titania cross her Oberon? I do but beg a little changeling boy to be my henchman. (*He points to the Indian child.*)

TITANIA   Set your heart at rest. The fairy land buys not the child of me. His mother was a votaress of my order . . .

OBERON   Give me that boy!

TITANIA   Not for thy fairy kingdom! Fairies, away!

With a screaming and rushing sound Titania and her train vanish from the glade.

OBERON   Well, go thy way; thou shalt not from this grove till I torment thee for this injury. My gentle Puck, come hither . . . (*Puck approaches, Oberon whispers in his crooked ear.*) Fetch me that flower, the herb I showed thee once; the juice of it on sleeping eyelids laid will make or man or woman madly dote upon the next live creature that it sees. Fetch me this herb!

PUCK   I'll put a girdle round about the earth in forty minutes!

Like a whirling leaf, Puck flies off. Oberon smiles.

OBERON   Having once this juice I'll watch Titania when she is asleep, and drop the liquor of it in her eyes; the next thing then she, waking, looks upon—be it on lion, bear or wolf, or bull, on meddling monkey, or on busy ape—she shall pursue it with the soul of love—

He is disturbed by a sudden crashing of branches. Instantly, he becomes invisible. The crashing grows louder and first Demetrius, then Helena, burst into the glade.

DEMETRIUS   I love thee not, therefore pursue me not! Where is Lysander and fair Hermia? Hence, get thee gone, and follow me no more.

HELENA   (*clutching tearfully at him*) I am your spaniel; and Demetrius, the more you beat me, I will fawn on you. Use me but as your spaniel, spurn me, strike me, neglect me, lose me; only give me leave, unworthy as I am, to follow you!

DEMETRIUS   (*flinging her off*) I am sick when I do look on thee!

HELENA   (*clutching him again*) And I am sick when I look not on you!

DEMETRIUS   Let me go, or, if thou follow me, do not believe but I shall do thee mischief in the wood!

He escapes and plunges away into the wood. Helena follows, weeping. Oberon becomes visible again.

OBERON   Fare thee well, nymph. Ere he do leave this grove, thou shalt fly him, and he shall seek thy love.

Puck returns, as swiftly as he departed. He kneels at his master's feet, and holds up a purple flower. Oberon takes it and gazes at it, musingly.

OBERON   I know a bank where the wild thyme blows, where oxlips and the nodding violet grows, quite over-canopied with luscious woodbine, with sweet musk-roses and with eglantine. There sleeps Titania some time of the night . . . (*He peers into the depths of the flower.*) With the juice of this I'll streak her eyes, and make her full of hateful fantasies. (*Puck laughs delightedly. Oberon frowns. He takes a petal from the flower and gives it to Puck.*) Take thou some of it, and seek through this grove: a sweet Athenian lady is in love with a disdainful youth; anoint his eyes; but do it when the next thing he espies may be the lady. Thou shalt know the man by the Athenian garments he hath on.

PUCK   Fear not, my lord, your servant shall do so.

Another part of the moonlit wood: the 'bank where the wild thyme blows'. Titania reclines upon a mossy couch. Her attendants watch over her, and her Indian boy plays happily . . .

TITANIA   Come now, a roundel and a fairy song . . .

ATTENDANTS

You spotted snakes with double tongue,
Thorny hedgehogs be not seen;
Newts and blindworms do no wrong,
Come not near our fairy queen . . .

As they sing, Titania closes her eyes and sleeps. The attendants creep away, taking with them the Indian boy. Titania is alone. Suddenly Oberon appears. He smiles, and, bending over his sleeping queen, squeezes the magic liquor from the flower upon her eyelids.

OBERON   What thou seest when thou dost wake, do it for thy true love take. Wake when some vile thing is near.

Slowly, Oberon vanishes. Titania sleeps on, 'quite over-canopied with luscious woodbine'. Slowly, she fades into invisibility. Into the glade, arm in loving arm, come Hermia and Lysander. They are plainly weary from walking.

LYSANDER   We'll rest us, Hermia, if you think it good.

HERMIA   Be it so, Lysander; find you out a bed, for I upon this couch will rest my head.

She seats herself. Lysander promptly sits beside her, very close.

LYSANDER   One turf shall serve as pillow for us both.

HERMIA   Nay, good Lysander; for my sake, my dear, lie further off yet.

He retires, but not by much. Hermia gestures urgently.

HERMIA   Lie further off, in human modesty; such separation as may well be said becomes a virtuous bachelor and a maid. (*Lysander at last betakes himself to a satisfactory distance.*) So far be distant; and good night, sweet friend.

They both settle down and, in moments, are asleep. No sooner are their eyes closed than Puck appears.

PUCK   There is he my master said despised the Athenian maid; and here the maiden, sleeping sound, on the dank and dirty ground. Pretty soul, she durst not lie near this lack-love, this kill-courtesy! (*He bends over Lysander and anoints his eyes with juice from the magic flower.*) Churl, upon thine eyes I throw all the power this charm doth owe.

Sounds of a violent approach cause Puck to vanish abruptly. Into the glade rushes Demetrius, followed by the weeping, brush-torn Helena.

DEMETRIUS   I charge thee, hence, and do not haunt me thus!

He plunges on, Helena pauses, and stares fearfully about her.

HELENA   O wilt thou darkling leave me? (*Suddenly she spies Lysander.*) But who is here? Lysander on the ground? Dead, or asleep? I see no blood, no wound. Lysander, if you live, good sir, awake!

She bends low over him, and gently shakes him. He opens his magically anointed eyes. Instantly he falls in love with Helena. He looks towards the sleeping Hermia. He frowns and shakes his head. He looks again at Helena, now radiant in his eyes.

LYSANDER   Not Hermia, but Helena I love: who will not change a raven for a dove!

He rises and tries to embrace her. Helena leaps back with a squeal of alarm.

HELENA   Good troth, you do me wrong, good sooth, you do! Fare you well!

She flies from the glade in great distress. Lysander stares at the sleeping Hermia. His expression is far from loving.

LYSANDER   Hermia, sleep thou there, and never mayest thou come Lysander near! (*He gazes after the departed Helena.*) All my powers, address your love and might, to honour Helen and to be her knight!

He pursues Helena. Hermia is left alone. She stirs and frowns, in the grip of a bad dream. She cries out in her sleep—

HERMIA   Help me, Lysander, help me! Pluck this crawling serpent from my breast! (*She wakes.*) Ay me, for pity! What a dream was there! (*She looks about her.*) Lysander! Lysander, lord! Alack, where are you! (*She rises and rushes from the glade.*)

For a moment, the place is quiet; then comes the tramp of sturdy feet and, one by one, the Athenian workmen, bearing their scrolls, enter the glade.

QUINCE   Here's a marvellous convenient place for our rehearsal.

BOTTOM   (*consulting his scroll*) Peter Quince, there are things in this comedy of Pyramus and Thisbe that will never please. First, Pyramus must draw a sword to kill himself, which the ladies cannot abide.

STARVELING   I believe we must leave the killing out, when all is done.

BOTTOM   Not a whit; I have a device to make all well. Write 'em a prologue, and let the prologue seem to say we will do no harm with our swords, and that Pyramus is not killed indeed; and for the more better assurance, tell him that I, Pyramus, am not Pyramus, but Bottom the weaver: this will put them out of fear.

QUINCE   Well, it shall be so. But there is two hard things: that is, to bring moonlight into a chamber; for, you know, Pyramus and Thisbe meet by moonlight.

BOTTOM   Why, then, you must leave a casement of the great chamber window, where we play, open—

QUINCE   Ay, or else one must come in with a bush of thorn and a lantern, and say he comes to disfigure, or to present the person of Moonshine. (*All nod wisely.*) Then there is another thing: we must have a wall in the great chamber; for Pyramus and Thisbe (says the story) did talk through the chink of a wall.

SNOUT   You can never bring in a wall. What say you, Bottom?

BOTTOM   Some man or other must present Wall; and let him have some plaster, or some loam, or some rough-cast about him to signify Wall.

QUINCE   If that may be, then all is well. Come, sit down every mother's son, and rehearse your parts. Pyramus, you begin . . .

They disperse themselves about the glade. Puck appears, in grinning invisibility.

PUCK   What hempen homespuns have we swaggering here, so near the cradle of the Fairy Queen? (*He stays to observe.*)

QUINCE   Speak, Pyramus! Thisbe, stand forth!

Bottom and Flute confront one another.

BOTTOM   Thisbe, the flowers of odious savours sweet—

QUINCE   Odorous—odorous!

BOTTOM   . . . odorous savours sweet. So hath thy breath, my dearest Thisbe dear. (*Quince thumps on the ground, as a cue.*) But hark, a voice. Stay thou but here awhile, and by and by I will to thee appear. (*Exit Bottom into a bush, above which hovers Puck.*)

FLUTE   Must I speak now?

QUINCE   Ay, marry, must you!

FLUTE   (*girlishly*) Most radiant Pyramus, most lily-white of hue! I'll meet thee, Pyramus, at Ninny's tomb.

QUINCE   At Ninus's tomb, man! Why, you must not speak yet; that you must answer to Pyramus. You speak all your part at once, cues and all! (*He turns to the bush*) Pyramus, enter! Your cue is past—

As he speaks, Puck, still hovering above the bush, makes a magic pass with his hands. A pair of large, hairy ears appears, poking through the leaves.

QUINCE Pyramus, enter!

A loud thumping, and Bottom emerges from the bush. But a strangely altered Bottom. In place of his human head is now the head of an ass!

BOTTOM If I were fair, Thisbe—

Bottom's companions stare at him in stark terror.

QUINCE O monstrous! O strange! We are haunted! Pray, masters! Fly, masters! Help!

They fly madly from the glade, leaving the weirdly altered Bottom alone.

BOTTOM Why do they run away?

Briefly, Quince returns, as if to make sure of what he has seen.

QUINCE Bless thee, Bottom, bless thee! Thou art translated! (*He departs.*)

BOTTOM I see their knavery: this is to make an ass of me, to fright me if they could . . . (*He begins to walk up and down, to keep his spirits up.*) I will sing, that they shall hear I am not afraid:

> The ousel cock, so black of hue,
> With orange-tawny bill,
> The throstle with his note so true,
> The wren with little quill . . .

As he sings, Titania, sleeping on her mossy couch, becomes visible. Skilfully, Puck leads the singing Bottom towards the Fairy Queen. Titania awakes, and feasts her magically anointed eyes upon the donkey-headed Bottom.

TITANIA What angel wakes me from my flowery bed? I pray thee, gentle mortal, sing again: mine ear is much enamoured of thy note. So is mine eye enthralled to thy shape, and thy fair virtue's force perforce doth move me on first view to say, to swear, I love thee.

Bottom gazes at the Fairy Queen without surprise; indeed, it would take much to surprise Bottom.

BOTTOM   Methinks, mistress, you should have little reason for that. And yet, to say the truth, reason and love keep little company nowadays. The more the pity that some honest neighbours will not make them friends.

Titania's attendants look on in amazement at this mad infatuation of their mistress. Titania rises from the ground and takes Bottom by the arm.

TITANIA   Thou art as wise as thou art beautiful.

BOTTOM   Not so neither; but if I had wit enough to get out of this wood, I had enough to serve mine own turn.

TITANIA   Out of this wood do not desire to go. Thou shalt remain here, whether thou wilt or no. I am a spirit of no common rate; and I do love thee: therefore go with me. I'll give thee fairies to attend on thee.

She signs to her followers, who obediently attend on Bottom. They all leave the glade, leaving behind the forgotten little Indian boy.

Another part of the wood. Oberon and Puck are together. Puck is helpless with laughter.

PUCK   My mistress with a monster is in love!

OBERON   This falls out better than I could devise. But hast thou yet latched the Athenian's eyes with the love-juice?

PUCK   I took him sleeping—

They are interrupted by the entry of Hermia, amorously pursued by Demetrius. Instantly, Puck and Oberon become invisible.

OBERON   Stand close; this is the same Athenian.

PUCK   This is the woman, but not this the man.

HERMIA   Out, dog; out, cur! Hast thou slain him then?

DEMETRIUS I am not guilty of Lysander's blood!

HERMIA   See me no more, whether he be dead or no!

She flies from him.

DEMETRIUS There is no following her in this fierce vein . . .

He sighs and sinks to the ground. He sleeps. Oberon and Puck reappear. Oberon remonstrates.

OBERON   What hast thou done? Thou hast mistaken quite, and laid the love-juice on some true love's sight. About the wood go swifter than the wind, and Helena of Athens look thou find!

PUCK   I go, I go, look how I go! Swifter than arrow from the Tartar's bow!

With a rush of leaves, as of a sudden wind, Puck flies off. Oberon bends over the sleeping Demetrius and anoints his eyes with liquor from the magic flower.

OBERON   Flower of this purple dye, hit with Cupid's archery, sink in th' apple of his eye. When his love he doth espy—

Puck returns, mightily out of breath.

PUCK   Captain of our fairy band, Helena is here at hand.

Oberon and Puck become invisible as the weeping Helena, still followed by the ardent Lysander, comes into the glade. Helena almost falls over the sleeping Demetrius, who wakes and, seeing her, instantly falls in love with her.

DEMETRIUS   O Helen, goddess, nymph, perfect, divine!

He tries to embrace her. Alarmed, she backs away . . . into the waiting arms of Lysander! She cries out and frees herself. She stares, tearfully, from one young man to the other.

HELENA	O spite! O hell! I see you are all bent to set against me for your merriment! You are both rivals, and love Hermia—
DEMETRIUS	Lysander, keep thy Hermia! If ere I loved her, all that love is gone, and now to Helen is it home returned!
LYSANDER	Helen, it is not so—
DEMETRIUS	Look where thy love comes; yonder is thy dear!

Enter Hermia. She rushes to Lysander.

HERMIA	Lysander, why unkindly didst thou leave me so?
LYSANDER	(*pushing her away*) Why seek'st thou me? Could not this make thee know the hate I bear thee made me leave thee so?
HERMIA	Hate me? Wherefore? Am I not Hermia? Are not you Lysander?
LYSANDER	Ay, by my life; and never did desire to see thee more. Be certain, nothing truer—that I do hate thee and love Helena.

Hermia stares at Helena, who, flanked by her two new lovers, smiles feebly.

HERMIA	You juggler! You canker-blossom! You thief of love!
HELENA	Have you no modesty, no maiden shame? You puppet, you!
HERMIA	Puppet? Thou painted maypole!

She launches herself furiously upon Helena, who skips behind the young men.

HELENA   Let her not hurt me! O, when she is angry, she is keen and shrewd. She was a vixen when she went to school!

HERMIA   Let me come at her!

LYSANDER   Get you gone, you dwarf!

He tries to comfort the terrified Helena. Demetrius pushes him aside. Lysander draws his sword. Demetrius does likewise. They circle each other, and, still threatening, back out of the glade. Hermia and Helena glare at each other.

HERMIA   You, mistress—

HELENA   (*backing away*) Your hands than mine are quicker for a fray; my legs are longer, though, to run away!

She bolts from the glade. Hermia pursues. Oberon and Puck reappear.

PUCK   Lord, what fools these mortals be!

OBERON   This is thy negligence; still thou mistak'st, or else commits thy knaveries wilfully.

PUCK   Believe me, king of shadows, I mistook.

OBERON   Thou seest these lovers seek a place to fight. Hie therefore, Robin, overcast the night . . . and lead these testy rivals so astray, as one come not within another's way . . . till o'er their brows death-counterfeiting sleep with leaden legs and batty wings doth creep. (*He gives Puck another flower.*) Then crush this herb into Lysander's eye . . .

As Puck, with magic signs, overcasts the night, a thick black fog begins to invade the wood, turning the trees to ghosts and the bushes to crouching bears. Lysander and Demetrius, no longer able to see one another, stumble on, while Puck taunts each of the rivals with the other's voice. At last, they collapse on the ground, quite overcome with weariness. Similarly, Helena and Hermia, pursued and pursuer, sink down and fall asleep. Puck, his work all but done, bends low over Lysander, and crushes the herb upon his eyelids.

PUCK   When thou wak'st, thou tak'st true delight in the sight of thy former lady's eye; and the country proverb known, that every man should take his own, in your waking shall be shown. Jack shall have Jill, naught shall go ill . . .

Puck gazes at the four sleeping lovers then fades away.

In Titania's glade, the Fairy Queen is entertaining her fantastical love. Donkey-headed Bottom, wreathed in flowers, reclines in Titania's arms, while her attendants gently fan him and tickle his hairy ears. The Indian boy plays on his own.

TITANIA   Sweet love, what desir'st thou to eat?

BOTTOM   Truly, a peck of provender; I could munch dry oats. (*He yawns.*) But I pray you, let none of your people stir me; I have an exposition of sleep come upon me.

TITANIA   Sleep thou, and I will wind thee in my arms. O how I love thee! How I dote on thee!

The attendants steal away as the strange lovers sleep. Oberon appears, with Puck. He looks with pity on the unnatural scene. He sees the Indian boy. He nods to Puck, who bears the child away.

OBERON   Now I have the boy, I will undo this hateful imperfection of her eyes . . . (*He squeezes the herb into Titania's sleeping eyes.*) Be as thou wast wont to be; see as thou wast wont to see . . .

Titania opens her eyes.

TITANIA   My Oberon! what visions have I seen! Methought I was
            enamoured of an ass!

OBERON   There lies your love!

*Titania, seeing the sleeping Bottom, shudders. Puck returns.
Oberon nods, and Puck restores Bottom to his proper human
shape. Titania seems unimpressed by the improvement.*

PUCK   Now when thou wak'st, with thine own fool's eyes peep.

OBERON   Come, my queen, take hands with me . . .

*Oberon and Titania join hands, and, with Puck and all their
returning attendants, dance away. Bottom is left alone, fast
asleep and smiling.*

Now that the creatures of the night have gone, thin arrows of daylight begin to pierce the wood. There are sounds of hunting horns, and hounds baying. Duke Theseus, with Hippolyta and courtiers, all attired for the hunt, appear.

THESEUS   The music of my hounds!

HIPPOLYTA   I was with Hercules and Cadmus once, with hounds of Sparta. I never heard so musical a discord, such sweet thunder.

THESEUS   My hounds are bred out of the Spartan kind; so flew'd, so sanded; and their heads are hung with ears that sweep away the morning dew; slow in pursuit; but matched in mouth like bells, each under each. A cry more tuneable was never hallooed to nor cheered with horn— (*He sees the four lovers, still sleeping.*) But soft, what nymphs are these?

Hermia's father, Egeus, is of the company. Angrily he examines the sleepers.

EGEUS   My lord, this is my daughter here asleep. And this Lysander; this Demetrius is, and this Helena.

THESEUS   Go bid the huntsmen wake them with their horns. (*Obediently, the horns bray out. The lovers awake in some confusion. They see the duke, and at once rise and kneel before him.*) I pray you, all stand up.

They stand, Lysander with Hermia, and Demetrius with Helena. Egeus tries to drag his daughter away from her love. She will not come. Egeus points furiously at Lysander, and addresses the duke.

EGEUS   I beg the law, the law upon his head!

Theseus gazes at the four lovers, and smiles.

THESEUS   Fair lovers, you are fortunately met. Egeus, I will overbear your will; for in the temple, by and by, with us, these couples shall eternally be knit. (*Egeus bows his head and resigns himself to the duke's decree.*) Away with us, to Athens: three and three, we'll hold a feast in great solemnity.

Theseus and his followers leave the glade. The four lovers gaze wonderingly at one another.

DEMETRIUS   These things seem small and indistinguishable, like far-off mountains turned into clouds.

HERMIA   Methinks I see these things with parted eye, when everything seems double.

HELENA   So methinks . . .

DEMETRIUS   Are you sure that we are awake? It seems to me that yet we sleep, we dream. Do not you think the Duke was here?

LYSANDER   And he did bid us follow to the temple.

DEMETRIUS   Why, then, we are awake. Let's follow him, and by the way let us recount our dreams.

In the glade once inhabited by the Fairy Queen lies Bottom, still asleep. Then he, too, awakes, with a start.

BOTTOM   When my cue comes, call me and I will answer. My next is, 'most fair Pyramus—' (*He stops and stares about him.*) Peter Quince? Flute, the bellows-mender? Snout, the tinker? Starveling? God's my life! Stolen hence and left me asleep! (*He touches his head, and fumbles uneasily for his ears. Finding them to be human ears, he sighs with relief.*) I have had a most rare vision. (*He gazes towards the mossy couch upon which he lay with Titania. He smiles.*) I have had a dream . . . I will get Peter Quince to write a ballad of this dream; it shall be called 'Bottom's Dream', because it hath no bottom . . .

Back in Athens, in their smoky, candlelit room, Peter Quince and his companions are sorely distressed.

QUINCE   Have you sent to Bottom's house?

STARVELING He cannot be heard of.

FLUTE   If he come not, the play is marred . . .

QUINCE   You have not a man in all Athens able to discharge Pyramus but he.

SNUG   If our sport had gone forward, we had all been made men.

FLUTE   O sweet bully Bottom! Thus hath he lost sixpence a day during his life. Sixpence a day in Pyramus, or nothing.

Even as they all mourn the loss of their chief hope, their star of stars, the door bursts open and Bottom himself stands in the doorway. Panting from running, he surveys his fellows, beaming proudly.

BOTTOM   Where are these lads? Where are these hearts?

QUINCE   Bottom! O most courageous day! O most happy hour!

BOTTOM   Get your apparel together! Every man look o'er his part; for the short and the long is, our play is preferred! Let Thisbe have clean linen, and let not him that plays the lion pare his nails. And, most dear actors, eat no onions nor garlic, for we are to utter sweet breath. No more words. Away!

In the royal palace, Theseus and Hippolyta, seated in state and attended by courtiers, await the night's entertainment.

HIPPOLYTA   'Tis strange, my Theseus, that these lovers speak of.

THESEUS   More strange than true. The lunatic, the lover, and the poet are of imagination all compact. One sees more devils than vast hell can hold; that is the madman. The lover, all as frantic, sees Helen's beauty in a brow of Egypt. The poet's eye, in a fine frenzy rolling, doth glance from heaven to earth, from earth to heaven, and as imagination bodies forth the forms of things unknown, the poet's pen turns them to shapes, and gives to airy nothing a local habitation and a name. Such tricks hath strong imagination—

HIPPOLYTA   But all the story of the night told over, and all their minds transfigured so together, more witnesseth than fancy's images, and grows to something of great constancy; but howsoever, strange and admirable.

The four lovers enter, and Theseus bids them seat themselves and prepare to be entertained. Philostrate, the Master of Revels, steps forward.

PHILOSTRATE   A play there is, my lord, some ten words long, which is as brief as I have known a play; but by ten words, my lord, it is too long.

THESEUS   What are they that do play it?

PHILOSTRATE   Hard-handed men that work in Athens here, which never laboured in their minds till now.

THESEUS   I will hear that play; for never anything can be amiss, when simpleness and duty tender it.

Philostrate bows and withdraws. Presently he ushers in Peter Quince and his company. They are all in costume, even to the man in the moon and the wall.

QUINCE   Gentles, perchance you wonder at this show; but wonder on till truth make all things plain. This man is Pyramus, if you would know; this beauteous lady Thisbe is certain; this man with lime and rough-cast, doth present Wall, that vile wall which did these lovers sunder; this man with lantern, dog and bush of thorn, presenteth Moonshine. This grisly beast, which Lion hight by name . . .

Great applause for the lion. The action of the play commences.

THESEUS   Pyramus draws near the wall; silence!

Bottom, attired as Pyramus, creeps towards Snout, the Wall.

BOTTOM   Thou wall, O wall, O sweet and lovely wall, show me thy chink to blink through with mine eye.

Snout's two fingers are raised for Bottom to blink through.

BOTTOM   No Thisbe do I see! Cursed be thy stones for thus deceiving me!

THESEUS   The wall, methinks, being sensible, should curse again.

BOTTOM	No, in truth sir, he should not. 'Deceiving me' is Thisbe's cue.

Enter Flute, attired as the lady Thisbe.

FLUTE	O wall, full often hast thou heard my moans—
BOTTOM	I see a voice; now will I to the chink, to spy and I can hear my Thisbe's face. Thisbe!
FLUTE	My love!
BOTTOM	Wilt thou at Ninny's tomb meet me straightway?
FLUTE	Tide life, tide death, I come without delay.

They exit gracefully.

HIPPOLYTA	This is the silliest stuff that ever I heard.
THESEUS	The best in this kind are but shadows; and the worst are no worse, if imagination amend them.

A tomb has appeared on the stage. Flute enters cautiously, accompanied by Moonshine, in the person of Starveling with his lantern, bush and dog.

FLUTE   This is old Ninny's tomb. Where is my love?

Enter Snug, as the lion. He roars fiercely. Thisbe squeals and flies, dropping her mantle.

DEMETRIUS   Well roared, lion!

THESEUS   Well run, Thisbe!

Lion savages Thisbe's mantle, leaving it bloody, then departs.

THESEUS   Well moused, lion!

Cheers and applause, and much laughter.

Enter Bottom. He sees the bloody mantle. He exhibits wild despair.

BOTTOM   What dreadful dole is here? Eyes, do you see? How can it be? O dainty duck, O dear! Thy mantle good—What, stained with blood? O Fates, come, come! Come, tears, confound! Out sword, and wound the pap of Pyramus; cry that left pap, where heart doth hop.

He draws his sword and prepares to extinguish himself.

THESEUS   This passion would go near to make a man look sad.

HIPPOLYTA   Beshrew my heart, but I pity the man.

BOTTOM   Thus die I, thus, thus, thus. (*Stabs himself repeatedly, and falls.*) Now am I dead, now am I fled; my soul is in the sky. Moon take thy flight. (*Exit Starveling, with his lantern, bush and dog.*) Now die, die, die, die.

Bottom, with many twitches, jerks, convulsions and groans, dies. Huge applause. Bottom rises, bows in acknowledgement, and lying down, gives an encore of his death agonies. At last, and most reluctantly, he becomes still. Flute enters, and beholds the recumbent Bottom.

FLUTE   Asleep, my love? What, dead, my dove? O Pyramus, arise. Speak, speak! Quite dumb? Dead, dead? Come, trusty sword, come blade, my breast imbrue. (*After vainly attempting to wrest the sword from Bottom's death-grasp, Flute stabs himself with the scabbard.*) Thus Thisbe ends—Adieu, adieu, adieu! (*Dies.*)

THESEUS	Moonshine and Lion are left to bury the dead.
DEMETRIUS	Ay, and Wall, too.

Bottom rises.

BOTTOM	No, I assure you, the wall is down that parted their fathers. Will it please you to see the epilogue, or to hear a Bergomask dance?
THESEUS	No epilogue, I pray you; for your play needs no excuse. Never excuse. But come, your Bergomask; let your epilogue alone.

The company bow, and the dance begins. As they dance, the court begins to rise, and, still applauding, the audience drifts away. At last, Bottom and his companions are alone, and at the end of their dance. They look at one another with great satisfaction, shake hands, and depart. Now the great hall is empty and dark. A bell begins to toll midnight. There comes a glimmering of tiny lights; then Oberon, Titania, Puck and all their fairy attendants troop in, each holding up a tiny glowing lamp.

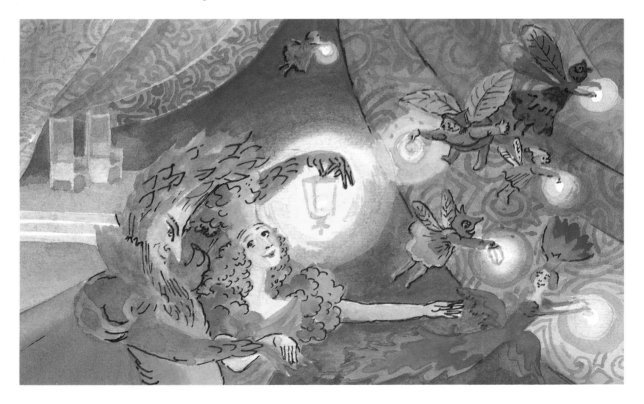

OBERON   Through the house give glimmering light . . . Sing and dance it trippingly . . .

The fairies begin to disperse, making strange patterns with their glowings.

TITANIA   Hand in hand with fairy grace, will we sing and bless this place.

OBERON   Now, until the break of day,
Through this house each fairy stray.
To the best bride-bed will we,
Which by us shall blessed be.

The fairies repeat the song as they begin to vanish into the deeper recesses of the palace.

OBERON   Trip away, make no stay; meet me all by break of day.

Oberon and Titania vanish in the wake of the vanishing lights. Puck alone remains. Then he grins and he too vanishes.

The curtain falls . . .